THE UNIVERSITY OF TEXAS®
LONGHORNS®
COOKBOOK

BARBARA BEERY
PHOTOGRAPHY BY ZAC WILLIAMS

GIBBS SMITH
TO ENRICH AND INSPIRE HUMANKIND
Salt Lake City | Charleston | Santa Fe | Santa Barbara

First Edition
12 11 10 09   10 9 8 7 6 5 4 3 2

Published by
Gibbs Smith
P.O. Box 667
Layton, Utah 84041

Orders: 1.800.835.4993

Designed and produced by Dawn DeVries Sokol
Printed and bound in China

Library of Congress Cataloging-in-Publication Data

Beery, Barbara, 1954-
   University of Texas Longhorns cookbook / Barbara Beery ; photographs by Zac Williams. — 1st ed.
      p. cm.
   ISBN-13: 978-1-4236-0495-2
   ISBN-10: 1-4236-0495-4
   1. Cookery, American—Southwestern style. 2. Cookery—Texas. 3. Texas Longhorns (Football
team) I. Texas Longhorns (Football team) II. Title.
   TX715.2.S69B44 2008
   641.59764—dc22
                                    2008014206

CONTENTS

Texas Toast
CHEESY BREADSTICKS

Ingredients

1 cup grated Mexican cheese blend

½ teaspoon smoked or sweet paprika

¼ teaspoon garlic powder

8 slices Texas Toast, crusts removed

¼ cup butter, melted

¼ cup chopped cilantro for garnish (optional)

Makes 24

Preheat a grill pan or fry pan to medium-low heat 5 minutes before grilling.

Toss together cheese, paprika, and garlic powder in a medium-size mixing bowl. Set aside.

Brush each bread slice lightly on both sides with melted butter.

Grill bread slices on each side until lightly toasted, about 30 to 45 seconds per side.

Sprinkle seasoned cheese equally over top side of grilled toasts. Cover with foil for about 1 minute to allow cheese to melt.

Remove covering and place each grilled toast on a cutting board. Allow to cool about 1 minute, and then slice each toast into three equal breadsticks.

Garnish with chopped cilantro if desired.

GRILL 'EM, HORNS!

Armadillo
POTATOES

Ingredients

¼ **cup panko breadcrumbs**

¼ **cup grated Parmesan cheese**

1 **tablespoon smoked or sweet paprika**

Salt and pepper, to taste

1–2 **tablespoons olive oil**

6 **Idaho potatoes, peeled and cut in half lengthwise**

Optional Garnishes

Ketchup

Bacon bits

Sour cream

Makes 12

Preheat oven to 450 degrees F. Line a sheet pan with foil and set aside. Cut 12 foil squares large enough to wrap each armadillo potato half (approximately 6 x 6 inches) and spray lightly with nonstick cooking spray.

In a medium-size bowl, mix together breadcrumbs, cheese, paprika, salt, pepper, and olive oil. Set aside.

Transform each potato half into a Texas armadillo by cutting nine notches that are ½ to 1 inch deep in the rounded top of each potato half.

Place each notched potato on a foil square, flat side down. Sprinkle the top with some crumb mixture and gently press it into the notches. Fold foil loosely around the potato then seal the aluminum foil completely where the ends meet. Arrange potatoes on prepared sheet pan and bake for 40 to 45 minutes.

Remove from oven and cool on pan for 5 minutes. Very carefully open the pouches as they will be steaming hot. Serve with garnishes if desired.

BAKE 'EM, HORNS!

Lone Star
QUESADILLAS

Ingredients

Olive oil cooking spray

1 box Spanish rice mix

Chicken broth

**10 whole wheat or
flour tortillas**

**1 can (15 ounces)
refried beans**

**1¼ cups grated Longhorn
cheddar cheese**

Garnishes

Shredded iceberg lettuce

Chopped tomatoes

Guacamole

Makes 5

COOK 'EM, HORNS!

Preheat oven to 375 degrees F. Line a sheet pan with foil and spray lightly with olive oil cooking spray. Set aside.

In a medium saucepan, cook the rice according to package directions, replacing water with chicken broth. Remove from heat and let cool for a few minutes while preparing tortillas.

Using a cookie cutter or sharp knife, cut tortillas into star shapes. Place 5 tortillas on prepared sheet pan; set 5 aside. Spread 1 to 2 tablespoons refried beans over one side of each tortilla on pan leaving about a ½-inch border around the edge. Spread about ¼ cup rice over the refried beans, and then sprinkle ¼ cup grated cheese evenly over rice.

Top each of the 5 tortillas with a remaining tortilla star. Press down lightly to adhere the two tortillas. Spray the top of each quesadilla lightly with olive oil cooking spray.

Place sheet pan in oven and bake for 10 to 12 minutes, or until tortillas are very lightly browned and cheese is beginning to "ooze" out from the sides of the quesadillas. Remove from oven and cool a few minutes. Garnish and serve.

Chicken Fried
CHICKEN FINGERS

Ingredients

1½ cups flour

1 teaspoon seasoning salt

1 teaspoon pepper

1 teaspoon poultry seasoning

2 teaspoons paprika

½ teaspoon powdered cumin

½ teaspoon garlic powder

1 egg, beaten

½ cup milk

1 tablespoon lemon juice

1 pound chicken breast strips

1 cup canola oil

Serves 4

FRY 'EM, HORNS!

Line a sheet pan with foil and set aside. Line a second sheet pan with 3 to 4 layers of paper towels. Set aside.

With a whisk, stir together the first seven ingredients in a medium-size mixing bowl. In another bowl, combine egg, milk, and lemon juice.

Dip chicken breast strips into seasoned flour, then egg mixture, and then back into seasoned flour. Place coated chicken strips on foil-lined sheet pan and refrigerate uncovered for 30 minutes.

Heat oil in a fry pan over medium-high heat for 5 minutes. Remove chicken strips from refrigerator and, with tongs, carefully place 2 to 3 chicken strips into pan, making sure strips do not touch each other. Be careful—hot oil can splatter! Turn each strip over after about 1 to 2 minutes and cook on the other side for another 1 to 2 minutes, or until golden brown.

Using tongs, carefully remove chicken strips from pan and place on sheet pan with paper towels to drain. Repeat until all strips have been cooked.

Serve warm or at room temperature with white gravy, Ranch dip, honey mustard sauce, or ketchup. Refrigerate any uneaten chicken strips for later.

Little Longhorn
MEATBALL SLIDERS

Ingredients

3–4 tablespoons extra
   virgin olive oil

1 package frozen
   meatballs

12 dinner rolls

Sauce

2 cups ketchup

¼ cup mustard

¼ cup brown sugar

¼ teaspoon salt

¼ teaspoon pepper

Garnishes

1½ cups grated Longhorn
   cheddar cheese

12 sliced dill pickles

Preheat oven to 350 degrees F. Line a rimmed sheet pan with foil and pour the olive oil onto pan. Tilt pan to coat the bottom with oil. Set aside.

Place 12 meatballs on prepared sheet pan and place in preheated oven. Bake according to package directions. Remove pan from oven. Cut dinner rolls in half and toast them in the oven.

In a microwave-safe bowl, combine all ingredients for the sauce and heat on high for 30 seconds. Stir and heat another 10 to 15 seconds. Remove from microwave and set aside.

Place each meatball on bottom half of a toasted dinner roll. Ladle with sauce, and garnish with cheese and a pickle. Replace top half of roll and serve.

COOK 'EM, HORNS!

Makes 12

Texas "T"
TACO SALAD

Ingredients

- **1 cup sour cream**
- **1 cup salsa**
- **½ cup chopped fresh cilantro**
- **2 pounds Texas lean ground beef**
- **1 envelope taco seasoning mix**
- **Chicken broth**
- **1 head iceberg lettuce, shredded**
- **1 bunch green onions, chopped**
- **1 red bell pepper, seeded and chopped**
- **2 medium tomatoes, chopped**
- **1 cup canned black beans, drained and heated**
- **2–3 cups grated Longhorn cheddar cheese**
- **12 bags individual serving-size Fritos**

Combine sour cream, salsa, and cilantro in a medium-size mixing bowl. Transfer to a serving bowl. Keep covered in refrigerator until serving time.

Sauté beef in a large skillet over medium-high heat until browned, stirring to crumble. Drain off fat. Stir in taco seasoning, substituting chicken broth for water called for on package. Reduce heat and simmer 5 minutes, stirring occasionally. Place taco beef mixture in a large bowl.

On a large serving tray, pile up lettuce, onions, and bell pepper. Set aside. Put tomatoes, beans, and cheese into separate serving bowls.

Cut open each bag of Fritos lengthwise and across to form a "T." Place each bag on a plate and fold the cut wrapper back to expose the chips. Let guests pile on their own toppings as desired!

PILE IT UP, HORNS!

Serves 12

Beggin' for Bevo
KABOBS

Ingredients

- ½ **pound Texas boneless lean beef, cut into 1-inch cubes**
- ½ **pound fresh boneless, skinless chicken breasts, cut into 1-inch cubes**
- **Olive oil cooking spray**
- **3 tablespoons olive oil**
- **2 tablespoons Worcestershire sauce**
- ½ **teaspoon salt**
- ¼ **teaspoon pepper**
- **1 teaspoon smoky paprika**
- **1 clove garlic, smashed and minced**
- ½ **teaspoon grill seasoning**
- **12 (6-inch) wooden skewers**

Makes 12

Preheat oven to broil 10 minutes before ready to use. Line a sheet pan or broiler pan with foil and spray with olive oil cooking spray. Set aside.

In a large ziplock plastic bag, combine olive oil, Worcestershire sauce, salt, pepper, paprika, and garlic. Seal shut and shake well to blend ingredients. Open bag and add beef and chicken. Close bag and shake to coat meat and chicken with marinade.

Place sealed bag in a large bowl in the refrigerator and marinate for at least 30 minutes and up to 4 hours.

Soak skewers in a dish of hot water for about 30 minutes. Thread marinated chicken and beef onto skewers in equal amounts. Discard leftover marinade.

Place kabobs on prepared sheet pan and broil, about 3 to 4 inches below the heating element, for 5 to 7 minutes, turning kabobs over after about 3 minutes.

GRILL 'EM, HORNS!

Hook 'em
CORN DOGS

Ingredients

8 beef or turkey hot dogs, cut in half crosswise

1 package purchased breadstick dough or cornbread twists

16 craft or Popsicle sticks

Preheat oven to 375 degrees F. Line a sheet pan with foil and lightly spray with nonstick cooking spray. Set aside.

Insert a stick into the cut end of each hot dog half. Wrap each hot dog with breadstick or cornbread dough.

Place hot dogs on prepared sheet pan and bake for 15 minutes, turning over once halfway through baking time. Remove from oven and serve with ketchup or mustard.

HOOK 'EM, HORNS!

Makes 16

Orange-and-White
CHILI

Ingredients

- 3 pounds Texas top sirloin, chili-ground or cut into ¼-inch pieces
- 3 tablespoons bacon drippings or olive oil
- 4 large cloves garlic, minced
- 1 medium yellow onion, finely chopped
- 3 cups beef broth
- 1 cup tomato sauce
- 1 teaspoon onion powder
- 3 tablespoons chili powder
- 1 tablespoon sweet paprika
- 1 teaspoon oregano flakes
- 1 teaspoon ground cumin
- 1 teaspoon salt
- ½ teaspoon pepper
- 1–2 whole jalapeño or serrano peppers, seeded and halved

In a Dutch oven or large cook pot, brown the meat in the bacon drippings or olive oil. Add the garlic and onion and cook until just transparent, about 5 minutes.

Stir in beef broth and tomato sauce. Bring to a boil over medium heat. Add remaining ingredients and stir well to blend. Reduce heat to low and simmer, covered, for 1 hour.

Check chili occasionally to make sure that liquid covers the meat. If it begins to look dry, lower the heat and add a little more beef broth. After 1 hour, remove from heat.

Garnish each bowl of chili with a sprinkling of chopped orange bell peppers, a dollop of sour cream, and chopped cilantro if desired.

FIRE 'EM UP, HORNS!

Garnishes

**2 orange bell peppers,
  seeded and diced**

2 cups sour cream

**Chopped fresh cilantro
  (optional)**

★ ★ ★

Serves 6–8

BBQ Chicken
NACHOS

Ingredients

3 chicken breasts, cooked and shredded

1 cup BBQ sauce

¼ teaspoon Liquid Smoke

2 tablespoons finely chopped white onion

¼ cup chopped pickled jalapeños, drained

1 bag (6.75 ounces) tortilla chips

2 cups grated Longhorn cheddar cheese

Optional Condiments

1 cup halved cherry or grape tomatoes

1 cup shredded iceberg lettuce

½ cup salsa

½ cup sour cream

1 cup guacamole

Preheat oven to 400 degrees F.

In a large bowl, toss chicken with BBQ sauce and Liquid Smoke. Stir in onion and jalapeños. Set aside.

Arrange chips on a sheet pan that has been lined with foil and lightly sprayed with nonstick cooking spray.

Top chips with BBQ chicken mixture and then sprinkle cheese over top. Bake 8 to 12 minutes, or until cheese is melted and bubbly. Carefully remove from oven.

Serve hot topped with condiments as desired.

SMOKE 'EM, HORNS!

Serves 4–6

23

Big Tex Skillet
CORNBREAD

Ingredients

½ cup butter

1 cup yellow cornmeal

1 cup flour

1 tablespoon baking
powder

½ teaspoon salt

1 to 2 tablespoons sugar

¾ cup heavy cream

1 egg, beaten

¾ cup grated Longhorn
cheddar cheese

1 to 2 jalapeños, chopped
(optional)

Makes 8 slices

Preheat oven to 425 degrees F.

Put butter in a 9- to 10-inch cast-iron or ovenproof skillet and place skillet on a sheet pan. Heat in oven 5 to 10 minutes until butter has completely melted. Remove from oven and carefully tilt pan so butter coats the entire inside of pan. Set aside.

In a large bowl, combine cornmeal, flour, baking powder, salt, and sugar. Mix together with a whisk or fork. Make a well in the center of the dry ingredients and add the cream, egg, and melted butter from skillet. Mix with a spoon or spatula until all ingredients are just moistened.

Spoon half the batter into the skillet. Top with grated cheese and jalapeños if using. Pour in the remaining batter over top and smooth it carefully to cover cheese and jalapeños.

Place skillet back onto sheet pan and bake for 20 to 25 minutes, or until the cornbread is golden brown. Remove from oven and cool in skillet 10 minutes before slicing and serving.

BAKE 'EM, HORNS!

Crrrrunch 'em
HORNS TRAIL MIX

Ingredients

1 cup halved or coarsely chopped pecans

2 cups wheat, rice, or corn cereal

1 teaspoon cinnamon

3 tablespoons brown sugar

2 cups dried peaches, chopped

1 cup white chocolate chips

1 cup orange M&M's

Preheat oven to 350 degrees F. Line a sheet pan with foil and lightly spray with nonstick cooking spray. Set aside.

Combine pecans, cereal, cinnamon, and brown sugar in a mixing bowl. Toss ingredients using your hands and then turn out onto prepared sheet pan.

Spread mixture evenly over the sheet pan and bake for 10 minutes. Remove from oven and cool on pan for at least 10 minutes.

When nut-and-cereal mix is completely cool, transfer to a large serving bowl and add the peaches, chocolate chips, and M&M's.

TOSS 'EM, HORNS!

Makes 6-7 cups

Big Bertha
SNACK CUPS

Ingredients

1 green bell pepper, washed and dried

1 yellow bell pepper, washed and dried

1 orange bell pepper, washed and dried

1 red bell pepper, washed and dried

Assorted vegetables, nuts, pretzels, and cheeses

Assorted dips

Using a small serrated knife, cut each bell pepper in half lengthwise. Clean out seeds and inner membrane.

Using the serrated knife, cut a thin sliver of pepper off the bottom of the snack cup. Now it will sit without wobbling.

Fill each cup with assorted vegetables, nuts, pretzels, cheeses, and dips, such as Silver Spurs Ranch Dip (see page 35) or Go Longhorns Cheese Dip (see page 36).

CRUNCH 'EM, HORNS!

Makes 8

28

The Eyes of Texas
TAILGATE SALSA

Ingredients

3 tablespoons chopped white onion

½ cup fresh cilantro, chopped

2 cloves garlic, chopped

2 cans (14 ounces each) stewed tomatoes

2 serrano or jalapeño chiles, seeded and chopped

½ teaspoon salt

Pepper to taste

Place onion, cilantro, garlic, tomatoes, chiles, salt, and pepper in a blender or food processor. Blend until salsa reaches desired consistency. Serve with your favorite tortilla chips or the Spicy Tortilla Chip Strips (see page 32).

MIX IT UP, HORNS!

Makes 4 cups

Spicy Tortilla
CHIP STRIPS

Ingredients

8 Southwestern-flavored flour or corn tortillas

Olive oil cooking spray

½ teaspoon chili powder

¼ teaspoon ground cumin

2 teaspoons salt

Preheat oven to 350 degrees F. Line two sheet pans with foil. Set aside.

Cut each tortilla into thin strips with kitchen scissors. Divide strips equally between pans. Spray strips with olive oil cooking spray and toss to coat both sides.

In a small bowl, combine chili powder, cumin, and salt. Sprinkle evenly over tortilla strips.

Bake both pans in oven at the same time, until strips are just crisp, about 6 to 10 minutes. Remove from oven.

Serve with assorted dips and salsas. They are also great for topping chili or tortilla soup.

CRUNCH 'EM, HORNS!

Serves 4–6

Silver Spurs
RANCH DIP

Ingredients

**1 container (16 ounces)
sour cream**

**1 tablespoon white
vinegar**

**2 tablespoons minced
fresh parsley**

**2 tablespoons minced
fresh dill**

½ teaspoon garlic powder

**2 tablespoons freshly
grated onion**

Salt and pepper, to taste

In a small bowl, mix together the sour cream and vinegar until smooth. Add the parsley, dill, garlic powder, onion, salt, and pepper. Cover and refrigerate for at least 1 hour or up to 2 days.

Serve in Big Bertha Snack Cups (see page 28) with Spicy Tortilla Chip Strips (see page 32) and assorted veggies for dipping.

MIX IT UP, HORNS!

★ ★ ★

Makes about 3 cups

Go Longhorns
CHEESE DIP

Ingredients

8 ounces cream cheese, softened

2 cups grated Longhorn cheddar cheese

½ cup plain yogurt

¼ teaspoon garlic powder

1 tablespoon freshly grated onion

¼ teaspoon salt

¼ teaspoon pepper

1 jar (14 ounces) pimientos, drained

Place cream cheese in a medium-size mixing bowl and beat with a hand mixer on medium speed for about 3 minutes, or until cream cheese is whipped and fluffy.

Add cheddar cheese, yogurt, garlic powder, onion, salt, and pepper. Stir to combine ingredients. Fold in pimientos.

Store in a covered container in the refrigerator until ready to use. Serve with crackers, chips, or fresh veggies.

WHIP 'EM, HORNS!

★ ★ ★

Makes about 4 cups

Forever Longhorn
CARAMEL DIP

Ingredients

- ½ **cup butter**
- 1 **cup firmly packed brown sugar**
- ½ **cup heavy whipping cream**
- ½ **teaspoon ground cinnamon**
- 1 **tablespoon vanilla**

Heat butter in a medium-size saucepan over medium heat until melted. Add brown sugar and cream and stir to blend. Bring to a boil, stirring occasionally.

Remove from heat and stir in cinnamon and vanilla.

Serve warm or at room temperature as a dip for apple slices, other fresh fruit, and marshmallows. It's also perfect on vanilla ice cream and southern pound cake. May be stored covered up to 3 days in the refrigerator and reheated before serving.

MELT 'EM, HORNS!

★ ★ ★

Makes about 2 cups

Texas Fight
PECAN TASSIES

Pastry Crust

1 cup butter, softened

1 package (6 ounces)
cream cheese, softened

2 cups flour

½ teaspoon ground
cinnamon

Pecan Filling

2 eggs

2 tablespoons butter,
melted

1½ cups firmly packed
brown sugar

¼ teaspoon salt

2 teaspoons vanilla

1 cup Texas pecans,
chopped

For the pastry crusts, combine butter and cream cheese in a medium-size bowl. Add flour and cinnamon, mixing well. Cover and chill dough in the refrigerator for about 1 hour.

Remove from refrigerator and shape into small 1-inch balls. Place each dough ball into an ungreased mini muffin pan cup. With your fingers, press each ball into the muffin cup, pushing it gently up the sides a little.

Place the pastry crusts in the refrigerator to chill while making the filling. Preheat oven to 375 degrees F.

For the filling, combine eggs, melted butter, brown sugar, salt, and vanilla in a medium-size bowl. With a whisk, beat well until smooth and thoroughly combined. Fold in chopped pecans.

Spoon about 2 teaspoons filling into each pastry-lined muffin cup. Bake for 20 to 25 minutes, or until pastry is golden brown and filling is set. Remove from oven and cool in pan for 10 minutes, then remove to a wire rack to cool completely.

★ ★ ★

Makes about 36

BAKE 'EM, HORNS!

Longhorn
CUPCAKES

Cupcakes

3 cups flour

1 teaspoon baking soda

1 teaspoon baking powder

¼ teaspoon salt

2 teaspoons cinnamon

¼ teaspoon pumpkin pie spice

2 cups sugar

1 cup canola oil

3 eggs

2 teaspoons vanilla

4 cups canned pumpkin*

4 ounces white chocolate chips

Frosting

2 containers purchased cream cheese frosting

Assorted orange and white candies or sprinkles

Tiny Longhorn mascots (optional)

not pumpkin pie filling

Preheat oven to 350 degrees F. Line muffin cups with cupcake liners.

With a whisk, combine flour, baking soda, baking powder, salt, cinnamon, and pumpkin pie spice in a large mixing bowl.

Add sugar, oil, eggs, and vanilla and beat with a hand mixer on low speed for 2 minutes.

Use a large spoon to fold in canned pumpkin and white chocolate chips.

Equally divide batter among muffin cups, filling about two-thirds full. Bake for 25 to 30 minutes, or until a toothpick inserted in a cupcake comes out clean. Remove from oven and allow cupcakes to cool on a wire rack for about 30 minutes before frosting.

To make frosting, combine both containers of prepared frosting in a large bowl. Add vanilla and stir well to blend. Generously mound and swirl frosting on top of each cupcake. Decorate with candies or sprinkles and novelty Longhorn mascots if desired.

WHIP 'EM, HORNS!

Makes 24

43

Texas Cowboy
COOKIES

Ingredients

3 cups flour

1 tablespoon each baking powder and baking soda

1 tablespoon ground cinnamon

1 teaspoon salt

1½ cups butter

1½ cups sugar

1½ cups firmly packed brown sugar

3 eggs

2 tablespoons vanilla

3 cups milk chocolate chips

3 cups old-fashioned rolled oats*

2 cups flaked coconut

2 cups pecans, chopped

*not quick-cooking oats

Makes 24

Preheat oven to 350 degrees F. Line three sheet pans with foil and spray lightly with nonstick cooking spray. Set aside.

With a whisk, combine flour, baking powder, baking soda, cinnamon, and salt in a large mixing bowl.

In another bowl, beat butter on medium speed until smooth and creamy, about 1 minute. Add both sugars and beat to combine. Add eggs, one at a time, beating well after each addition.

Stir in vanilla. Add flour mixture, 1 cup at a time, mixing by hand to combine. Stir in chocolate chips, oats, coconut, and pecans.

Drop dough, one-fourth cup at a time, onto prepared baking sheets, spacing 3 inches apart. Bake for 15 to 20 minutes, or until edges are lightly browned. Rotate sheet pans halfway through baking so cookies bake and brown evenly. Remove cookies from oven and cool on pans 10 minutes before removing to a wire rack.

BAKE 'EM, HORNS!

Big as Bevo
COOKIES

Cookies

½ **cup butter, softened**

¾ **cup sugar**

1 **egg**

1 **teaspoon vanilla**

¼ **teaspoon almond extract**

Orange paste or gel food coloring

2 **cups flour**

½ **teaspoon cinnamon**

½ **teaspoon baking soda**

½ **teaspoon salt**

Bevo-shaped cookie cutter

Icing

1 **container purchased vanilla frosting**

3 **tablespoons commercial meringue powder**

Makes 18-20

Preheat oven to 375 degrees F. Line two sheet pans with foil and spray lightly with nonstick cooking spray. Set aside.

Cream butter in a large mixing bowl; add sugar, beating until light and fluffy. Add egg, vanilla, almond extract, and orange food coloring. Mix well.

Add flour, cinnamon, baking soda, and salt; mix well to incorporate. Dough will be very stiff.

Divide dough in half. Cover dough not being used with plastic wrap to keep it from drying out and place in the refrigerator.

Roll out dough to about ½ inch thickness on a work area that has been lightly dusted with powdered sugar. Cut out cookies with Bevo-shaped cookie cutter. Place cookies 2 inches apart on prepared pans.

Bake for 10 to 12 minutes or until very lightly browned. Remove from oven and cool on pan for 5 minutes before removing to wire racks to cool another 10 minutes before icing.

To make icing, combine purchased frosting, meringue powder, and orange food coloring in a mixing bowl until smooth.

Spoon and spread about 1 tablespoon icing onto each cookie, placing each one back on wire rack to dry for a few minutes before creating the eyes, nose, and mouth of Bevo with decorator frosting, decorator gel, and candies.

Allow the decorated cookies to dry on wire rack for at least 1 hour before transferring to a storage container or serving.

Orange paste or
   gel food coloring
1 tube white decorator
   frosting
1 tube black decorator gel
Small chocolate-coated
   candies

BAKE 'EM, HORNS!

Ice Cream Cone
MEGAPHONES

Megaphones

12 sugar cones

1 pound vanilla candy coating or vanilla almond bark

1 tube orange decorator icing

Fillings

Popcorn

Small bite-size candies

Miniature marshmallows

Assorted chopped or small dried fruits

Makes 12

FILL 'EM, HORNS!

Line a sheet pan with foil and set aside. On your work area, place a large wire rack on a large sheet of foil the same size as the rack.

Melt the package of vanilla candy coating according to package directions. Set aside in a bowl to cool slightly for 5 minutes.

Take one cone at a time, open end down, and place it on the wire rack. Spoon about 4 tablespoons melted candy coating over the top. Start at the point of the cone and allow the coating to run down the sides. Smooth and spread candy coating to completely cover the cone. Repeat until all cones have been coated.

Cool for 15 minutes or until cones are dry to the touch. To dry cones more quickly, place rack with cones in the refrigerator for 5 to 10 minutes.

When coating has hardened, use the decorator icing to make the capital letters UT on each cone megaphone.

To serve, place ice cream cone megaphones on a serving tray. Have several bowls of assorted candies, popcorn, miniature marshmallows, and fruit available for friends to fill their megaphones with their favorite choices.

Lickety-Split
LONGHORN POPS

Ingredients

4 large ripe mangoes, peeled, pitted and roughly chopped

1 cup freshly squeezed orange juice

1 cup vanilla yogurt

¼ teaspoon almond extract

1 teaspoon freshly squeezed lime juice

10–12 craft or Popsicle sticks

½ cup white sprinkles

Makes 10–12

In a blender, combine all ingredients except white sprinkles until smooth and creamy.

Spoon mixture into paper cups, cover with squares of foil, and insert a craft or Popsicle stick into each cup. Or spoon into your favorite Popsicle molds. Freeze for 4 hours.

Remove Popsicles from cups or molds. Cover tops with sprinkles. Place on a sheet pan and put back in freezer for 15 minutes. Remove and serve immediately.

LICK 'EM, HORNS!

We're #1
PRETZEL RODS

Ingredients

24 (8 to 10-inch) pretzel rods

1 pound white candy coating or white almond bark

Orange and white candies and sprinkles

Line a sheet pan with foil and set aside.

Melt vanilla candy coating according to package directions.

Dip each pretzel rod into melted candy coating, generously covering half the pretzel. Or drizzle with candy coating instead of dipping.

Decorate with orange and white candies and sprinkles and place each on prepared sheet pan.

Place sheet pan with decorated pretzels in refrigerator to chill and harden for 15 minutes, or until ready to serve. Remove from refrigerator 10 minutes before serving.

DIP 'EM, HORNS!

Makes 24

Pennant
COOKIES

Cookies

¾ cup butter, softened

½ cup firmly packed
  brown sugar

1 egg

¾ cup molasses

3 cups flour

¼ teaspoon salt

2 teaspoons ginger

1 teaspoon cinnamon

½ teaspoon cloves

½ teaspoon nutmeg

Powdered sugar for
  rolling out dough

10–12 medium length
  pretzel sticks

Makes 10–12

In a large bowl, combine butter, brown sugar, egg, and molasses. Stir in flour, salt, and spices and mix completely. Remove dough from bowl and place in a large ziplock bag. Refrigerate for 2 to 3 hours or overnight.

Preheat oven to 350 degrees F. Line two sheet pans with foil and spray lightly with nonstick cooking spray. Set aside.

Remove chilled dough from refrigerator. Dust work area lightly with powdered sugar.

Work with only a small amount of dough at a time (about ½ cup) and roll out to ½ inch thickness. Keep the rest of the dough covered in the refrigerator until ready to roll out. Cut each section of dough into a narrow triangle approximately 4 to 5 inches long and 2 to 3 inches at the widest point to create the pennant shape. Continue until all dough is used.

Place cookies 2 inches apart on prepared pans and bake for 10 to 15 minutes or until lightly browned.

Remove cookies from oven and cool on sheet pan for 5 minutes, then carefully remove to a wire rack to cool another 10 minutes before frosting.

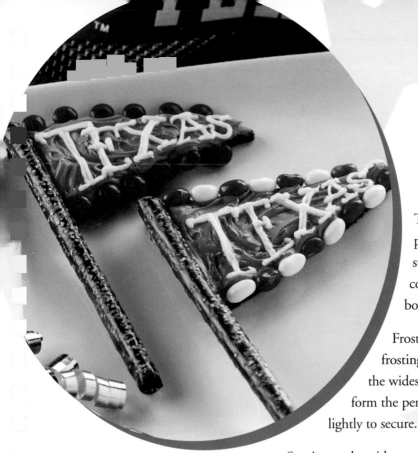

To make frosting, combine purchased frosting, powdered sugar, vanilla, and orange food coloring in a medium-size bowl. Stir well to blend.

Frost each cookie evenly with frosting. Press a pretzel stick onto the widest end of each cookie to form the pennant handle. Press down lightly to secure.

Starting at the widest end of the cookie, write in capital letters the word TEXAS with the decorator icing. Decorate with candies as desired.

ROLL 'EM, HORNS!

Frosting

1 can purchased vanilla frosting

½ cup powdered sugar

1 teaspoon vanilla

Orange paste or gel food coloring

1 tube white decorator icing

Orange and white candies

Pralines-and-Cream
ICE CREAM SUNDAES

Ingredients

1 pint vanilla ice cream, softened

1 teaspoon cinnamon

1 tablespoon brown sugar

1 recipe Forever Longhorn Caramel Dip (see page 39)*

½ cup Texas pecan halves

1 can whipped cream or whipped topping

4 maraschino cherries with stems

*1 jar (8 ounces) purchased caramel sauce may be substituted

Serves 4

Place softened ice cream in a large mixing bowl. Stir in cinnamon and brown sugar. Cover bowl and return to freezer for 15 minutes.

Spoon 1 to 2 tablespoons caramel in the bottom of each ice cream dish. Top with 2 or 3 pecan halves.

Remove ice cream from freezer and place one big scoop of ice cream on top of caramel and pecans. Spoon more caramel sauce and pecans on top.

Finish sundaes with a generous dollop of whipped cream and garnish each with a maraschino cherry.

TOP 'EM, HORNS!

Peachy Keen
COBBLER

Crust
½ cup butter

1 cup flour

1 cup sugar

2 teaspoons baking powder

¼ teaspoon salt

1 cup whole milk

Filling
4–5 cups sliced fresh peaches

2 teaspoons vanilla

½ teaspoon almond extract

Topping
½ cup sugar

½ cup firmly packed light brown sugar

½ teaspoon ground cinnamon

Serves 6–8

Preheat oven to 350 degrees F.

Melt the butter in a saucepan over medium heat. Remove from heat and pour into a 9 x 13-inch baking dish. Set aside.

Place flour, sugar, baking powder, and salt in a small mixing bowl. Blend with whisk to combine ingredients. Stir in milk using a mixing spoon. Pour batter directly over melted butter in prepared baking dish.

Combine peaches with vanilla and almond extract and gently toss to mix. Arrange peaches evenly over the batter.

In a separate bowl, combine sugars and cinnamon. Sprinkle evenly over peaches.

Place baking dish on a sheet pan and bake for 30 to 40 minutes until fruit is bubbling and crust is golden brown. Remove from oven and serve warm or at room temperature. Serve with vanilla ice cream or whipped cream if desired.

BAKE 'EM, HORNS!

Orange-and-White
CREAM SODAS

Ingredients

- **½ cup orange jimmies**
- **1 pint vanilla Bluebell brand ice cream***
- **1 liter Orange Crush, chilled****
- **1 can real whipped cream**

Any vanilla ice cream may be substituted

**Any orange soda may be substituted*

Makes 4

Line a small sheet pan with foil and set aside. Place jimmies in a small bowl.

Scoop out four portions of vanilla ice cream, about ½ cup each, and form into balls. Roll each ice cream ball in jimmies, making sure to cover the entire ball. Place ice cream balls on prepared sheet pan and place in the freezer for a few minutes while preparing the drink.

Squirt about 3 tablespoons of whipped cream into the bottom of four soda fountain glasses. Pour enough orange soda into each glass to fill about three-fourths full.

Remove ice cream balls from freezer and place one into each soda-filled glass. Serve immediately.

SCOOP 'EM, HORNS!

COLLECT THEM ALL!

BARBARA BEERY is an Austin native and a graduate of The University of Texas at Austin. Barbara founded Batter Up Kids in 1991 offering hands-on cooking classes and parties just for kids. She is a best-selling cookbook author, entrepreneur, and spokesperson and is always looking to stir up kid-friendly opportunities in the kitchen.

Super Sipping
SPORTS PUNCH

★ ★ ★

Makes 2 quarts

Ingredients

1 package unsweetened
orange Kool-Aid
drink mix

2 quarts cold water or
chilled sparkling water

¼ cup sugar

½ cup freshly squeezed
orange juice

⅛ teaspoon salt

MIX IT UP, HORNS!

Stir together all ingredients in a large punch bowl or pitcher. Serve with plenty of ice.